TO BE ALONE
Amajla Tricic

Dedicated to the girl I used to be

LUNA

No one is really alone
Not even the moon
Not even the darkest parts of it
Not even the far side of it

And we are no different
We are bound by atoms
Ones that are hopelessly attracted to each other
Elements forming and heat rising
The kind where two people love each other
And the warmth of their bodies collide

No one is really alone
Not even the moon
Not even the destroyed parts of it
Not even the oldest rock of it

And we are not dissimilar
We are the beginning of endings
The gravitational pull so powerful the stars explode
And the stardust emerges
They clump together to form a new genesis
We clump together and form a new life

The moon is not really alone
There are parts of us within her
The impact of Mother Earth
And the moon's own Mother Theia
Met halfway and gave life to the glowing Luna

We are all one

When the moon's face is looking down on us
She remembers we are looking up at her

WHO WE WERE

I was ten when I took a touristy trip down to Virginia Beach and received a shell encrusted jewelry box for my big two-digit birthday. God, it was so tacky. Clunky pink neutral shells invade it and I can barely still open the damn thing, let alone touch it. All the dust fills up my nostrils like they do the inside of the shell where you can still hear the ocean and the echoes of my family's laughter. Sometimes I think if I open it, I'll be back in the place where I never thought about my innocence and how easy it was for my dad to give me piggy back rides. I'm in the place where my mom used to rub Aloe Vera on my body because I didn't put sunscreen on when she told me to. She tells me I have to face the consequences, but her gentle touch tells me she wants the pain to go away. My cousins and I are watching movies that we are too young for and our parents think we are asleep. I'm watching my older sister be mischievous while the boys on the beach are looking at her. I think to myself, "I can't wait to be that cool and graceful one day", every day she becomes more graceful. Even now I still don't think I have figured it out myself. The clunky box from an overpriced gift shop resides on the corner of my vanity. Never really belonging in the scheme of my mess. But it stays. Sometimes I think if I open it, there will be a world I miss, but there's only rusted rings that are too loose for my fingers, and red satin lining covered in grime. It stays because the only thing I've truly got is what I can remember, and that damn hideous thing reminds me that I do want to remember.

A MOMENT FROZEN IN TIME

The rusted blue swing set barely clung to the dirt of the earth,
moving back and forth, up and down, when the swing reached
for the sky

But I was still happy

Sometimes my brother would jump so high off the swing he
would land headfirst, grazing that same dirt with his teeth

But he was still happy

My cousins and I would race each other up and down the yard
until the blue sky turned purple and the porch lights turned on,
wearing mud covered adidas sandals and hosed down shorts. My
brother would always win

But we were still happy

Sometimes we thought we could take our bikes to the forbidden
place that was the sidewalk in front of my two-story yellow
house. But we would only hear the shrieks of my mother from the
balcony telling us to go back before we even made it

But we were still happy

After the darkness cloaked the yard and the figures of children in
the night, we sulked inside where bursts of yellow light peeked
through the windows

But we were still happy

Mud-covered footprints found themselves on the hardwood
floors, cherry red popsicles waited in freezers, the warmth of a
bath, my mother's fingers against our scalps and cool floral
sheets were slept in

And we would always be happy

Because the rusted blue swing set waited for us when the dark
hues in the sky left

IT IS LONELY WHERE I AM

The blue in her veins never seemed to falter
Maybe because the white on her skin took notice of the things
That were important and made them apparent
She could have told you a million times
Nobreathbetweenhersentences of the things she felt
The voices in her head said it was a burden to share your pain
It was humiliating to not know why you felt it either
So, all she did was think and that almost helped destroy her
The only reminder she had was the blue in her veins
Her body's need to remind her was the only thing that helped
Her endure

SECRETS IN THE DARK

When the moon rose
You told me your mom lights up your life
I should have told you that you light up mine
That ever since you came around
My life has not known silence
My heart has not beat so fast
It has never felt so disposed
It has never soared so high

I told you that my father is my hero
You were eager to meet him
But you saw something in me too
You told me it was nice to just talk
And you were never one to share the good
Or talk about the bad
But you did with me

I could stay up all night with you
And catch up on my sleep when you are not around
But it's different in the morning
People will give you their poetry and tales in the dark
And then pretend like it never meant as much as it did
When the sun rises

SOMETIMES LOVE IS NOT ENOUGH

I know he makes you weak
Especially when he smiles
And the way he touches you
Or his voice in the morning

I know you want all of him

But it is not enough if he only wants parts of you

THINGS CHANGE AND YOU DO TOO

It wasn't until the one thing I truly loved came crashing down to earth that I found something that made me feel like the moon surrounded by stars

Sometimes your dreams die in order to let other dreams come to life

A MALIBU IN THE NIGHT SKY

You arrived when the sun was setting
And always left before the sun got a chance to rise

I don't know who you were during the day
But the night said I could have you all to myself

Flooded in darkness and drinks
We came alive

A malibu in the night sky told me
I could be anyone I wanted to be
And I decided to be yours

YOU HAVE YOURSELF

At my worst
My loneliness echoed my fears
It often traded my happiness with sorrow
Because loneliness wanted to be seen and heard

My loneliness told me to think about how feeble I am in this
universe
My loneliness made me anxious in the middle of the grocery
store aisle
My loneliness made me fall in love with the wrong person
Because my loneliness didn't want to be alone

At my best
My loneliness echoed my accomplishments
It reminded me that it is not a burden to be proud
Because loneliness wanted me to be seen and heard

My loneliness told me I am a part of this universe; I'm not just
looking at it
My loneliness told me sometimes I had to be scared before I
could be fulfilled (and that's okay)
My loneliness made me fall in love with myself
My loneliness found it wasn't alone because it had me

WOMEN ARE NOT ONE DIMENSIONAL

I had to spend years unlearning what it meant to be a woman

It was decided we were soft
Sensitive to the touch
Feminine to the core
Pastel pinks, blues, and yellows invaded us
Emotional and therefore could not be in charge
Dependent on a secure life, a secure man, a secure motherhood

I wanted to strip every part of that off of my body

It was decided I wanted to be strong
Thick-skinned and sharp-witted
Dark reds, purples, and blues conquered me
Owning my sexuality and embracing the skin I was given
A leader who was independent, alone, my only security

But no one ever told me I was allowed to be both

I am strong
I can bang my hands against my chest and demand for a better
world
But I am also vulnerable
I can cry of a broken heart and lay my head on my mother's chest
Despite that, I can still get my work done at the end of the day
It's okay that sometimes I am lost, confused, and scared
That doesn't make me any less powerful

I can have the fairytale ending and still be full of fire, focused, and self-supporting

I can raise a generation, raise myself, raise a business, raise the standards

I can be a wild one when I want to

But I can be quiet

I can have dreams that seem innocent and magical

But they'll turn into visions that are real and influential

You are not limited to your potential

You are not the archetype of a devil or an angel

You are a woman

STOP WAITING

You're always waiting for the big thing
Until you realize it's made up of small things

It was a habit of mine to hope for milestones
But no one ever told me it's already happening

COSMOS

You do not want anyone to be the sun for you
Be your own universe
Find your own galaxies
But don't go looking for stars
They all burn you
They all burn out

DO NOT FALL IN LOVE WITH ME

Do not fall in love with me
I will attach myself to you
And then I will leave
I will ask you why you don't talk to your father anymore
And then I will stop asking you if you are alright

Do not fall in love with me
I will tell you I want to see you
And then I will tell you I am tired goodnight
I will hold you closer so I can feel your warmth
And then I will sit on the opposite side of the couch
Suddenly you notice you are always cold

Do not fall in love with me
I will tell you I cannot imagine a life without you
But it is eight days later and I am fine
I will think about the way your lips feel on mine
And wipe the wetness of them right off of my own

Do not fall in love with me
I will love you until I can't anymore
Until I don't want to anymore

Do not fall in love with me
Simply because I cannot love anyone
As well as I can *love myself*

SMILE

You have a pretty face why don't you show that smile
I told him I don't need to smile for anyone
I am not a puppet on which you can pull the strings
I am a person
And I will not smile for his satisfaction

THINGS I LOVE

My dad's rough callused hands pressed against my cheek.

The orange and yellow hues of the sky when the sun falls and my family is laughing.

Writing in the dark at 2 am when my sorrow sinks into the keyboard.

Long road trips when I lay in my mom's lap and look up to see the blur of the trees.

My cold hands wrapped around hot coffee.

The beginning of a new year with kisses against cheeks and sweaty embraces.

Sheltered in a fuzzy blanket.

A chest as a pillow.

Desperate hands reaching for one another.

Warmth in the form of a human.

Him.

I AM HERE

I listened to the leaves rustle around me
Saw the sun's reflection rippling on the silver-blue lake
The scent of burnt wood and cold air prickled my body

I saw the world as it was
Engines roaring past
The rhythm of walking feet
Children's laughter

I spent all that time looking out into the world
Listening to other people's stories
Picturing what it was like to be the couple holding hands
The man who spent every weekend raking the leave
The little daughter being held in her father's arms

Why did I forget I was someone too
Rosy cheeks, yellow hair, lost face
In the backdrop of scarlet and gold leaves
I lost sight that I mattered just as much as the world moving
around me

The wood kept burning
The cold embraced me
The leaves crunched beneath my feet
And the sun beat down on my face and lit it up

THE WORLD IS WIDE WHERE I STAND

The world begins at my feet
And it never ends

That whatever was beyond where I stood
Whatever I dreamed
Whatever I craved
Whatever I loved
Would not take its daggered grey hands and rip it away from me
That there would not be a dead end ahead telling me to turn
around and go home

My possibilities didn't stop where I stood
They didn't stop if I kept walking to the ends of the earth
They didn't stop if I found myself in the stars

Because the world begins at my feet
And it tells me I am infinite

RESIST

People will build walls
But you can build bridges
Climb mountains
Knock down concrete barriers
And unite

The world is too precious for anything else.

I'M ONLY THAT GIRL FOR YOU

I never wanted to be that girl
Who tried so much for someone who only gave so little

But if I could ever do it again
I wouldn't think twice

No tears
No grief
No embarrassment
No shame

Could undo
The way you undid me

HAPPINESS IS NOT A DEFAULT SETTING

I don't think anyone can truly be happy
Not all the time, at least
You can't wake up and smell the roses
But you can lay there and question why you do anything at all
What makes us strong is that we get to feel a lot of things
And it feels damn good when we experience happiness
Even if it's for a second

IT WILL STOP RAINING

For a while, it poured rain and the lightning that accompanied it struck the ground so hard it made cracks and jagged lines that ended at my feet

No one noticed

After that, there were distant rumbles of thunder and steady showers

No one noticed

When it stopped, the earth was damp, there were puddles beneath me and the sun was able to peek through the clouds

No one noticed

Eventually, I was able to lay in a field of green and gaze upward to a color of blue, finally breathing in the roses, daffodils, sunflowers, and dirt

I had to put my soul back together and no one noticed

NOTHING'S GONNA CHANGE MY WORLD

Once, the thought of being small made me sad
I hated those videos that zoomed out of a city until all you saw
were eight tiny planets
Then it showed the Milky Way that holds all of them
Earth looked like a period at the end of my sentences

I realized the planet was small in the grand scheme of things
I realized how small I was
How small my problems were
How small my dreams were
And that we were all just specks of nothing
If we disappeared, the universe wouldn't care

But I also realized how vast we were or weren't didn't really
matter
And it didn't determine our significance in the universe
Maybe we do hold a purpose in the grand scheme of things
We are intertwined to make something bigger than us
Because what is the universe without the things in it

ONE STEP AHEAD

Maybe one day you woke up and finally felt okay after a long time

Or maybe one day you went through the day and realized today was better than yesterday

And maybe one day you didn't have a good day after having so many of them, that's okay too

But one day, when you least expect it, you'll feel really good

You're still one step ahead and that is all that matters

TO BE ALONE

To be alone is not to be lonely

Alone is the smell of Autumn when leaves are falling on dewy grass in the morning and the sun blinds the empty streets

Alone is a cup of hot coffee and a soft plush blanket covering your shoulders

Alone is the patter of rain against a window and a book that changes your life

Alone is driving mindlessly and listening to songs that make you remember how things used to be; you'll smile because you endured the past, missed it, cherished it and you'll always have it

Being alone means knowing who you truly are when no one is around

Amajla Tricic (Uh-My-La) (Treech-eech) is a preschool teacher who lives in New York with her two Guinea Pigs, Albus and Thor. She majors in English at Utica College and is a news editor for the school newspaper.

Made in the USA
Columbia, SC
24 August 2019